975.6
FOR

Foran Jill
North Carolina

34880000 823398

NORTH CAROLINA

Jill Foran

Published by Weigl Publishers Inc.
123 South Broad Street, Box 227
Mankato, MN   56002
USA
Web site: http://www.weigl.com

Library of Congress Cataloging-in-Publication Data available upon request from the publisher. Fax: (507) 388-2746 for the attention of the Publishing Records Department.

ISBN 1-59036-003-6

Printed in the United States of America
1 2 3 4 5 6 7 8 9 10   05 04 03 02 01

Editor
Michael Lowry
Copy Editor
Diana Marshall
Designers
Warren Clark
Terry Paulhus
Photo Researcher ·
Angela Lowen

Photograph Credits
Every reasonable effort has been made to trace ownership and to obtain permission to reprint copyright material. The publishers would be pleased to have any errors or omissions brought to their attention so that they may be corrected in subsequent printings.

Cover: Old Salem (Bruce Roberts), Shells (Corel Corporation); **Bettmann/CORBIS/MAGMA:** pages 17T, 18, 19; **Bruce Bennett Studios:** page 27; **Corel Corporation:** pages 3M, 10B, 11T, 11B, 14B, 26T, 28R; **Defense Visual Information Center:** page 15; **Digital Stock:** pages 28L, 29L, 29R; **Bruce Leighty:** pages 14T, 21T, 21B; **PhotoDisc Corporation:** page 25T; **Photofest:** page 25B; **Mississippi Department of Archives and History:** page 17B; **J & D Richardson:** pages 7B, 7T, 8B; **Bruce Roberts:** pages 3T, 3B, 4T, 4B, 6, 8T, 9T, 9B, 10T, 12T, 12B, 13T, 13B, 20T, 20B, 22T, 22B, 23, 24, 26B; **Marilyn "Angel" Wynn:** pages 16T, 16B.

CONTENTS

The Currituck Beach Lighthouse was the last lighthouse built on North Carolina's coast.

QUICK FACTS

The state flag was adopted in 1885. The flag must be displayed at all public buildings, state institutions, and courthouses.

The Outer Banks are a chain of sandy islands found along the coast of North Carolina.

Some of the houses along the Outer Banks have been constructed out of the hulls of old shipwrecks, while others are decorated with items rescued from sunken ships.

INTRODUCTION

Located on the Atlantic coast, North Carolina is a beacon of light for travelers of the high seas. The state's coastline is dotted with lighthouses—at least one every 40 miles. The lighthouses attempt to guide ships to safety around the treacherous Outer Banks. Situated on the Outer Banks, Cape Hatteras has one of the highest number of shipwrecks in the world, earning it the nickname "The Graveyard of the Atlantic." Today, scuba divers are drawn to the region to explore more than 2,000 sunken ships hidden beneath the ocean's surface.

North Carolina has earned itself another distinctive nickname—"The Tar Heel State." This name can be traced back to the American Civil War. During a battle in Virginia, Confederate soldiers from other states retreated, leaving North Carolina soldiers to fight Union forces alone. When the battle was over, the soldiers from North Carolina threatened to put tar on the heels of the other Confederate soldiers, so that they would be forced to stick their ground for the next battle.

The beaches along the Outer Banks are dotted with the remains of old shipwrecks, some of which date back to the 1500s.

Getting There

North Carolina is located in the southeastern United States, midway between New York and Florida. North Carolina is bordered by Virginia to the north and Tennessee to the west. South Carolina and Georgia border North Carolina to the south, and the Atlantic Ocean forms its long, eastern boundary.

There are many ways to get to North Carolina. Five major interstate highways run through the state, and a variety of secondary highways provide links to the state's towns and cities. Rail service is also available. Twelve passenger trains offer daily trips across the state. For those who prefer to fly, the state has three international airports and eleven regional airports. The Douglas International Airport in Charlotte, and the Raleigh-Durham International Airport are the state's busiest airports. Travelers can also reach North Carolina by boat. The state has ports along the Intracoastal Waterway, which is a protected sailing route along the Atlantic coast.

North Carolina Location Map

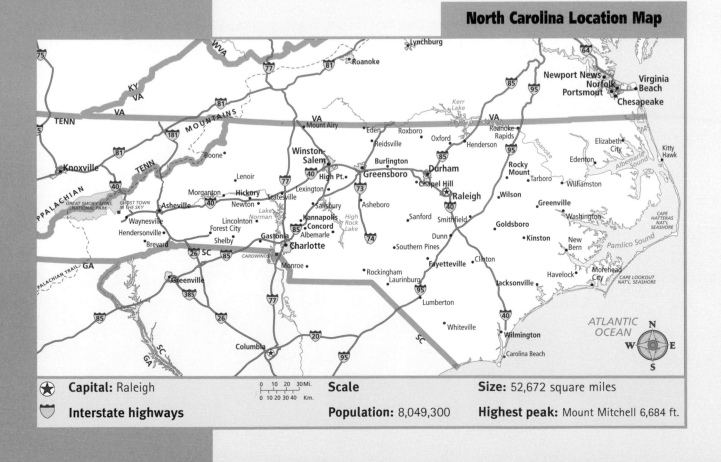

Capital: Raleigh

Interstate highways

Scale
0 10 20 30 Mi.
0 10 20 30 40 Km.

Size: 52,672 square miles

Population: 8,049,300

Highest peak: Mount Mitchell 6,684 ft.

After the American Revolution, North Carolinians were hesitant to join the Union. Citizens of the state did not like the idea of a strong federal government. In 1789, North Carolina finally agreed to join only after several changes were made to the Constitution.

Three United States presidents were born in North Carolina. Andrew Jackson was born in Waxhaw, James K. Polk was born in Mecklenburg County, and Andrew Johnson was born in Raleigh.

The state's official song is "The Old North State." The song was written by William Gaston and was adopted in 1927.

In the late sixteenth century, North Carolina became the location of the first English colony in North America. Founded in 1585, this early settlement seemed doomed from the beginning. The first settlers were unprepared for life in the New World and had returned to England by 1586. Another group of English settlers was sent to the same area in 1587, but by 1590, they had all mysteriously disappeared. These early tragedies did not prevent other Europeans from settling in North Carolina. By the late 1700s, there were close to 350,000 people living in the state. In 1775, North Carolinians joined the other states in the fight for independence from England, in the American Revolution.

By the mid-1830s, slavery was very much a part of North Carolina's economy. African-American slaves carried out the tasks of planting and harvesting the state's many crops. When northern states pressed to end slavery, southern states feared a loss of income and power. Tensions between the North and the South resulted in the American Civil War. Many Civil War battles took place in North Carolina, and the state suffered widespread destruction. After the Union won the war in 1865, slavery was **abolished** across the country.

American Civil War historical groups often re-enact the battles that took place in North Carolina.

More than 328,000 boats are registered in North Carolina.

QUICK FACTS

The eastern box turtle became North Carolina's official state reptile in 1979.

The official state gem is the emerald. In 1970, one of the largest emeralds in the world was found near Hiddenite. The emerald weighed 1,438 **carats** and was valued at $100,000.

The Plott hound was adopted as the official state dog in 1989. This breed of dog was once used to hunt wild boars in the Mountain Region.

Charlotte is considered one of the largest financial centers in the country.

North Carolinians rebuilt their state quickly after the war. By the end of the nineteenth century, agriculture and other industries were once again prosperous. On December 17, 1903, from high atop a towering sand dune near Kitty Hawk, called Kill Devil Hill, two brothers—Wilbur and Orville Wright—conducted the first successful airplane flight. The Wright brothers had been visiting North Carolina's sand dunes for 2 years prior to the flight. For those 2 years, they flew **prototype** kites and gliders made out of bicycle parts. These experiments led to the construction and operation of the world's first functional airplane.

Today, North Carolina continues to be a site of innovation. It is home to a number of thriving industries and has become a leader in manufacturing. The state is also known for its excellent research facilities, and its highly respected colleges and universities. These features, along with the state's beautiful scenery and friendly atmosphere, attract millions of new residents and visitors every year.

A monument to the Wright brothers' achievement was built on Kill Devil Hill in 1932.

Some of North Carolina's mountains are over a mile above sea level.

LAND AND CLIMATE

North Carolina can be divided into three natural land regions—the Atlantic Coastal Plain, the Piedmont, and the Mountain Region. The Atlantic Coastal Plain extends along the Atlantic Ocean. The Outer Coastal Plain consists of low islands, hazardous off-shore sand bars, grassy marshlands, large swamps, and shallow lakes. The Inner Coastal Plain features sand dunes, prairies, and some of the state's best farmland.

The Piedmont is located in the middle part of the state. It is made up of gently rolling hills. Much of North Carolina's manufacturing and most of its population are concentrated in this area. To the west of the Piedmont is the Mountain Region. It consists of steep mountain ranges and dense forests.

Average January temperatures range from 40° Fahrenheit to 45°F in most areas. In July, the average temperature in the mountains is 68°F, while the average temperature for the rest of the state is 84°F. During spring and fall, North Carolina's coast is often exposed to violent storms and hurricanes.

North Carolina has more than 300 miles of coastline.

North Carolina's forest resources supply lumber for the state's booming construction industry.

NATURAL RESOURCES

North Carolina's rich soil is one of the state's most important natural resources. The sandy soil, found in the western and central parts of the Atlantic Coastal Plain, is ideal for growing crops. The Piedmont also has productive soil. The most fertile soil in this region contains rich **alluvial** materials.

Trees are another important natural resource in North Carolina. Nearly 60 percent of the state is covered with forests that support a wide variety of wildlife and contribute to the thriving lumber industry. The state's many bodies of water are also significant natural resources. North Carolina's lakes, rivers, and coastal waters are teeming with fish and other marine life, helping to sustain a healthy fishing industry. Some of the state's rivers serve as sources of **hydroelectricity**.

North Carolinians catch almost $100 million worth of seafood every year.

QUICK FACTS

The pine tree grows abundantly in North Carolina and is the tree most commonly used for lumber. It became the official state tree in 1963.

North Carolina's fishing industry contributes more than $100 million to the state's yearly economy. The state's most valuable catches are blue crab, clam, shrimp, flounder, and trout.

More than 300 types of rocks and minerals can be found in North Carolina.

North Carolina's Pisgah National Forest is comprised of more than 500,000 acres of wooded wilderness.

QUICK FACTS

North Carolina has four national forests—Pisgah, Nantahala, Croatan, and Uwharrie. Together, these national forests cover more than 1.2 million acres.

North and South Carolina are the only places in the world that the Venus's-flytrap grows in the wild.

North Carolina has the largest variety of plant life of all the eastern states.

PLANTS AND ANIMALS

The dense forests of North Carolina's Mountain Region consist of maples, birches, beeches, hemlocks, firs, and spruces. Pine trees and hardwood trees grow in the Piedmont region. Loblolly pines and longleaf pines are found throughout the Atlantic Coastal Plain, while white cedars, black tupelos, and sweet gums grow in swamps and along rivers. The Atlantic Coastal Plain is recognized for its distinctive plant life. At least eleven **carnivorous** plants grow in the state's swampy areas. One of the most interesting of these is the Venus's-flytrap. This plant traps insects with its blade-hinged leaves and then digests them.

About 500 years ago, most of North Carolina was covered with forests. As settlers arrived in the area, many of these forests were cleared for agriculture or cut down by loggers. Soon, there was a need to protect the remaining forests. In 1898, a huge step in forest **conservation** was made in North Carolina when George Schenck founded the country's first school of forestry. Called the Biltmore Forest School, it trained students in forest management.

There are several different varieties of rhododendrons in North Carolina.

North Carolina is home to a wide range of animals. Deer are found throughout the state, while squirrels, rabbits, raccoons, opossums, and foxes inhabit the wooded areas. Black bears live in the western mountains and in parts of the Atlantic Coastal Plain. The coastal plain also serves as habitat for many reptile species, including the American alligator—the largest reptile in North America. Several thousand alligators live in the state's southeastern swamps and rivers.

Cardinals, Carolina wrens, mockingbirds, and woodpeckers are among North Carolina's most common birds. Wild turkeys, quails, and doves are also found in abundance. During winter months, many bald eagles can be seen in Uwharrie National Forest, at the Badin Lake and Tilley Lake **reservoirs**. The eagles are attracted to the easy fishing these reservoirs offer. Among the many fish species found in the state's lakes and rivers are trout, bass, perch, bluegill, and crappies. The coastal waters are home to sea trout, sharks, Atlantic croakers, blue crabs, and shrimps.

Black bears are found only in the eastern coastal plain and in the western mountains of North Carolina. They were once common throughout the state.

QUICK FACTS

A variety of snakes are found throughout North Carolina. Some of these snakes, such as the rattlesnake and the water moccasin, are poisonous.

Wildlife refuges, such as the Alligator River National Wildlife Refuge, work to protect the state's many threatened species.

The largest alligator found in North Carolina measured 12 feet 7 inches, from head to tail.

The beaches along the Atlantic coast are prime nesting grounds for loggerhead turtles.

The cardinal became North Carolina's official state bird in 1943. It lives in the state year-round.

Biltmore Estate is a popular attraction in Asheville. With more than 250 rooms, it is the largest home in the United States.

TOURISM

Every year, more than 9.3 million visitors make their way to Great Smoky Mountains National Park. It is one of the most visited parks in the country. The park covers 800 square miles and stretches over the border into Tennessee. Tourists travel to the park for outdoor activities, such as mountain biking, hiking, and camping.

Visitors to North Carolina can take scenic drives along the Atlantic coast. Many vacationers travel to the coast to enjoy the unspoiled beaches, quiet resort towns, and majestic lighthouses of the Outer Banks. In the summer, more than 3,000 visitors climb the stairs to the top of the Cape Hatteras Lighthouse each day. It is the most recognized and most frequently photographed lighthouse in North America.

Another popular historic site, in North Carolina, is the Wright Brothers National Memorial at Kitty Hawk. This memorial honors the outstanding achievements of the brothers. It sits near the site of their first successful motor-powered flight.

At 208 feet high, the candy-striped lighthouse at Cape Hatteras is the tallest in the country.

QUICK FACTS

Tourism in North Carolina adds about $12 billion to the state's economy every year.

During the winter, thousands of tourists from the northern states travel to North Carolina's Sand Hills for relief from the cold weather.

The Great Smoky Mountains are named for the blue haze that lingers over its vegetation. The "smoke" is caused by water vapor that is released by the plants into the air.

At Fort Raleigh National Historic Site, visitors can learn about the mysterious disappearance of the more than 100 early English settlers on Roanoke Island.

North Carolina harvests about 1.4 million bales of cotton per year.

INDUSTRY

Agriculture was North Carolina's most important industry up until the early twentieth century. Today, North Carolina remains the number one ranking tobacco farming state in the country. It also leads the United States in the production of tobacco products. Tobacco contributes close to $810 million to the state's economy every year. There are more than 40,800 tobacco farms in North Carolina, and approximately 255,000 people are employed by the tobacco industry.

Other North Carolina crops include corn, cotton, peanuts, soybeans, and sweet potatoes. The state's most important livestock includes broiler chickens, hogs, and beef cattle.

In the 1920s, manufacturing surpassed agriculture as the main economic activity. Since then, North Carolina has grown to become the second most industrialized state in the South, behind Texas. Manufacturing employs more than 856,000 North Carolinians.

There are more than 12,000 tobacco farmers in North Carolina.

QUICK FACTS

There are approximately 58,000 farms in the state. Farmland covers about 30 percent of North Carolina.

North Carolina has nearly 450 **textile** factories. These factories produce a variety of cloth materials, including hosiery, denim, and carpet. The textile factories in North Carolina produce more cloth materials than any other state.

North Carolina is a leading producer of sweet potatoes. More than 4 billion pounds of this vegetable are harvested each year.

The Research Triangle Park, near Raleigh, is a 7,000-acre research facility that contains the offices and laboratories of more than 130 major corporations.

North Carolina is the nation's leader in furniture production. Most Americans have North Carolina furniture in their homes.

GOODS AND SERVICES

Chemicals are among North Carolina's most profitable exports. Factories throughout the state produce goods, such as **pharmaceuticals**, **synthetic** fibers, plastics, and detergents.

North Carolina leads the country in the production of household furniture. High Point is nicknamed "The Furniture Capital of America." The city is home to more than 120 furniture factories, as well as the International Home Furnishings Center, the largest furniture market in the world.

Many of North Carolina's goods are exported to other states and countries. The state's excellent transportation system ensures quick and convenient shipment. Close to 80 percent of the freight in North Carolina is transported by the state's highways. The highways are so well maintained that the state is often called "The Good Roads State." North Carolina transports goods by rail as well. About twenty-five rail lines provide freight service to and from the state.

Cargo ships transport goods to and from major ports in North Carolina, such as the Port of Wilmington and the Port of Morehead City.

Close to 25 percent of the people employed in North Carolina work in one of the state's many service industries. These industries combine to contribute the most money to the state's economy. Law firms, insurance companies, hotels, restaurants, and malls are among the many types of employers in this sector. Government services, also considered part of this sector, include the operation of public hospitals, public schools, and military bases. Some of the country's largest military bases are located in North Carolina, including Fort Bragg, Camp LeJeune Marine Corps Base, and Seymour Johnson Air Force Base.

The University of North Carolina opened its doors at Chapel Hill in 1795, making it one of the first state universities in the country. Today, the university consists of sixteen campuses located in various cities, including Chapel Hill, Raleigh, and Charlotte. North Carolina has an extensive community college system. Made up of fifty-eight different institutions, it is one of the largest community college systems in the United States.

Soldiers take part in training exercises at Pope Air Force Base, near Fayetteville.

The Cherokee Indian Reservation, in western North Carolina, was founded in 1889.

FIRST NATIONS

More than 35,000 Native Peoples from thirty different groups were living in the North Carolina region when the first European explorers arrived. The Cherokee, who were the largest of North Carolina's early Native-American groups, inhabited the mountains that make up the western border of the state. Other major groups included the Catawba and the Hatteras.

North Carolina's early Native Peoples lived primarily in settled communities. The area's abundance of natural resources provided plenty of materials for food, clothing, and shelter. Many of the earliest Native-American homes were huts made of twigs, brush, and split cane, and were covered with bark. Later, these early huts were replaced with sturdier houses called "hogans." Hogans were constructed out of logs and covered with **sod** or hardened mud. When the weather turned cold, most groups stayed warm in buildings called "hothouses," which were built partly underground and covered with earth. This construction prevented heat from escaping.

Early Native-American lacrosse games would often last all day.

Giovanni da Verrazzano explored North Carolina's coast between Cape Fear and Kitty Hawk.

EXPLORERS AND MISSIONARIES

The first European known to have explored North Carolina's coast was an Italian named Giovanni da Verrazzano. In 1524, Verrazzano wrote a report that described all of his findings. This report was sent to King Francis I, of France, but the king made no attempt to colonize the region.

Spanish explorers were the next Europeans to explore North Carolina. In 1540, Hernando de Soto explored the mountains in the southwestern region, followed by Juan Pardo who explored them in 1566 and 1567. However, like the French, the Spanish made no attempt to settle the area.

England was the first European country to show interest in colonizing the North Carolina region. In 1584, Sir Walter Raleigh sent an expedition to choose a suitable site for a colony. When the explorers returned to England, they told Raleigh all about the Roanoke Island area, describing it with great enthusiasm.

Hernando de Soto was one of the first Europeans to explore North Carolina by land.

On August 18, 1587, John White's granddaughter was born on Roanoke Island. Named Virginia Dare, she was the first baby born to English parents in the United States.

When John White returned to Roanoke Island in 1590, he found the word "croatan" carved into a post, and "cro" carved into a tree. These carvings may have been clues explaining that the settlers had gone to live with a Native-American group called the Croatan. However, when White went in search of his colony, he did not find them.

North Carolina's first permanent group of English settlers came from Virginia in around 1650. They settled in the Albemarle Sound region.

EARLY SETTLERS

In 1585, Raleigh sent 108 settlers to establish a colony on Roanoke Island. By 1586, several misfortunes forced the colonists to return to England. Eighteen men stayed behind to protect England's claim to the land. In 1587, Raleigh sent a second group of settlers to Roanoke Island. Upon their arrival in July, all that was left of the eighteen men were a few skeletons.

By the end of August, the second group was running out of supplies. The governor of the colony, John White, had to sail back to England for more supplies. He was forced to stay in England for 3 years because the country's war with Spain kept him from sailing out of English ports. When White finally returned to Roanoke Island in 1590, there was no sign of life. The entire colony had mysteriously disappeared. Today, Roanoke Island is known as the "Lost Colony," and the disappearance of its settlers remains an unsolved mystery.

The settlers sent by Sir Walter Raleigh reached Roanoke Island in the summer of 1585.

During the 1600s and 1700s, settlers to North Carolina came from Virginia, as well as from European countries, such as France, Germany, and Switzerland.

The Tuscarora Indian War began in 1711. The Tuscarora were angry that European settlers had taken much of their land. They attacked several settlements and killed many settlers. The settlers fought back, and war raged on for the next 3 years. The colonists defeated the Tuscarora in 1713.

North Carolina was the site of the country's first gold rush. In 1799, the son of a German settler found gold in Little Meadow Creek.

Further attempts to settle the North Carolina region did not take place until the seventeenth century. In 1663, King Charles II, of England, granted the colony of Carolina to eight English noblemen, making them ruling landlords. These landlords divided Carolina into three counties—Albemarle, Clarendon, and Craven. A governor was appointed to each of the counties. When North Carolina became its own colony in 1712, it received its own governor.

During the late 1600s and 1700s, more and more settlers came to North Carolina. These new colonists suffered through many difficult times. They fought a violent war against the Tuscarora and were terrorized by pirates, such as Blackbeard, who took control of the coast. In 1775, North Carolina declared its independence from England. Many residents of the colony fought in the American Revolution. In 1789, 6 years after the war had ended, North Carolina became the twelfth state of the newly formed Union.

Blackbeard was killed by British soldiers off the coast of North Carolina in 1718. Blackbeard's real name was Edward Teach.

POPULATION

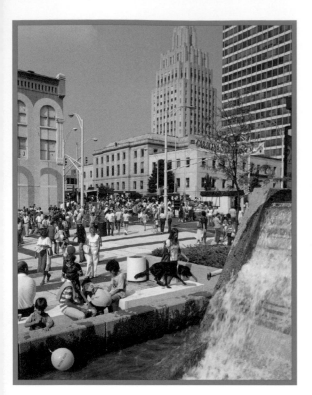

The population of Winston-Salem has grown by almost 30 percent since 1990. Today, the population is about 185,700.

North Carolina has one of the largest **rural** populations in the country. About half of the state's 8 million citizens live in rural areas. Of the state's three land regions, the Piedmont is home to the highest concentration of people. This region also contains North Carolina's six largest cities—Charlotte, Raleigh, Greensboro, Winston-Salem, Durham, and Fayetteville.

People of many different ethnic backgrounds call North Carolina home. Close to 72 percent of the population is of European heritage. These North Carolinians include those whose ancestors came from such countries as England, Ireland, Scotland, Germany, and Switzerland. African Americans make up about 22 percent of the state's population, while Native Americans make up more than 1 percent. Other cultural groups represented in the state include Asian Americans, Pacific Islanders, and Hispanic Americans.

QUICK FACTS

Many North Carolinians have been able to maintain a rural lifestyle because several of the state's industries are located in smaller towns or within easy commuting distance.

Between 1990 and 2000, North Carolina's population grew by 21.4 percent. During that decade, only eight other states grew faster than North Carolina.

Charlotte is the largest city in North Carolina. It was named after Queen Charlotte, the wife of England's King George III.

The city of Asheville, in Buncombe County, has a population of about 66,700.

The North Carolina State Capitol was completed in 1840.

POLITICS AND GOVERNMENT

North Carolina's government is divided into three branches. The legislative branch makes the state's laws. It consists of a 50-member Senate and a 120-member House of Representatives. Together, these groups are known as the General Assembly. All members of the General Assembly are elected to 2-year terms.

The executive branch of government makes sure that the state's laws are carried out. The governor heads this branch and is elected to a 4-year term. Other elected members of the executive branch include the lieutenant governor and eight administrative officers.

The third branch of North Carolina's government is the judicial. This branch ensures that North Carolina's laws are obeyed and is made up of several courts and judges. The highest court in the state is the Supreme Court.

The design of the Capitol, in Raleigh, is influenced by ancient Greek architecture.

North Carolinians celebrate their European roots at Old Salem, a restored historic village.

CULTURAL GROUPS

Many of North Carolina's cultural groups can trace their roots back to Europe. Germans arrived in North Carolina in the eighteenth century to farm the fertile land. The Moravians were Germans who had immigrated to Pennsylvania before settling in North Carolina. One of the first communities established by the Moravians was Salem, which was founded in 1766 and is now known as Old Salem. Today, Old Salem has been restored so that visitors can learn about eighteenth century Moravian life in North Carolina.

One of the largest Native-American reservations in the country is located on the western edge of North Carolina. It is home to the Cherokee and once served as a hideout for Cherokee who refused to leave the mountains when many of the state's other Native-American groups were forced to leave by the Europeans. Today, the Cherokee share their early heritage at the Oconaluftee Indian Village, which is located on the reservation. Visitors to the village can see typical Cherokee homes of the 1700s and watch Cherokee women weave baskets.

North Carolina's Cherokee Indian Reservation has more than 12,000 registered members.

African Americans are one of the largest and most prominent cultural groups in North Carolina. Many of the state's present-day African Americans are descended from the men, women, and children who were brought to the region as slaves over 200 years ago. Today, African Americans honor their heritage with events, such as Black History Month, and museums, such as the African American Cultural Complex.

During the 1960s, African Americans in North Carolina played an important role in the growing **civil rights movement**. On February 1, 1960, four African-American students formed a "sit-in" at a **segregated** Woolworth's restaurant in Greensboro. The students sat at the lunch counter all day and waited to be served. Throughout the week more people joined the sit-in, until the restaurant was forced to close its doors. Soon, sit-ins, like the one in Greensboro, spread across the South as a peaceful means of protest.

The Grandfather Mountain Highland Games celebrate Scottish culture in North Carolina.

QUICK FACTS

Winston-Salem State University is home to the Society for the Study of Afro-American History. This society has one of the most complete collections of information on African-American history and current events in the country.

The Mendenhall Plantation, in Jamestown, is home to one of only two remaining historic false-bottomed wagons. These wagons were used to help transport slaves to freedom in the 1800s.

The Scottish in North Carolina celebrate their heritage with the annual Highland Games and Gathering of Scottish Clans at Grandfather Mountain.

The North Carolina Symphony was one of the first state symphonies in the country. It was founded in 1943.

Many movies and television shows have been filmed in North Carolina. Among the most popular are the Teenage Mutant Ninja Turtles series, the *Indiana Jones Chronicles*, *Richie Rich*, and parts of *Forrest Gump*.

One of North Carolina's most popular theatrical performances is *The Lost Colony*. It is produced every summer at Fort Raleigh in Mateo. The play portrays the hardships and challenges faced by the early English settlers who tried to colonize Roanoke Island.

ARTS AND ENTERTAINMENT

North Carolina has produced a variety of talented artists and performers. Several North Carolina actors have achieved success in television and in the movies. One of the state's best-known actors is Andy Griffith. Griffith grew up in Mount Airy and starred in many popular television shows, including *The Andy Griffith Show* and *Matlock*. Another well-known actor from North Carolina is Pam Grier. Born in Winston-Salem, Grier has starred in several Hollywood films, such as *Mars Attacks* and *Snow Day*.

Many gifted visual artists live in North Carolina. One of these artists is Bob Timberlake, who is known for his beautifully detailed paintings. His paintings can be seen in museums across the country. The largest museum in the state is the North Carolina Museum of Art, in Raleigh. It features an enormous collection of art, ranging from ancient Egyptian pieces to contemporary works.

The Lost Colony has been performed in the Waterside Theater, at Fort Raleigh, every year since 1937.

North Carolina is home to a strong literary tradition. Several highly respected writers were born in the state. Novelist and playwright Thomas Wolfe was born in Asheville in 1900. One of his plays, *Welcome to our City*, was set in his hometown of Asheville. William Sydney Porter was another respected writer from North Carolina. Born in 1862, he wrote many short stories under the **pen name** O. Henry. These stories, which were known for their surprise endings, were widely read in the early part of the twentieth century.

Many celebrated musicians have come from North Carolina. Jazz pianist Thelonious Monk was born in Rocky Mountain, in 1918. He was an innovative jazz musician who is often credited with helping to create the unique jazz sounds of the 1940s. Jazz saxophonist John Coltrane was also from North Carolina. Born in 1926, Coltrane emerged in the 1950s as one of the most influential jazz performers of all time. Other musicians from the state include Grammy-Award winning singer Roberta Flack, folk singer James Taylor, and country performer Ronnie Milsap.

Authors from North Carolina have produced many great works of literature, including **Thomas Wolfe's** *Look Homeward, Angel.*

QUICK FACTS

The North Carolina Museum of Art was the first state-funded art museum in the country.

Rick Dees is originally from Greensboro. He is a **disc jockey** who hosts his own Weekly Top 40 radio show.

Author Maya Angelou was born in Arkansas, but she has lived in North Carolina since the early 1980s. Her most well-known work is *I Know Why the Caged Bird Sings.*

John Coltrane is credited with re-creating jazz music and influencing generations of musicians. Coltrane was born in Hamlet.

SPORTS

North Carolina's mountains and coasts provide residents with fantastic recreational opportunities. North Carolina's four national forests and sixty-three state parks offer a variety of hiking and mountain biking trails, as well as many other outdoor challenges. Rock climbers scale the vertical cliffs at Hanging Rock State Park, while hang gliders soar over massive sand dunes at Jockey's Ridge State Park.

For those who prefer water sports, the state's coastal areas are ideal for sea kayaking, windsurfing, surfing, and scuba-diving. The long stretches of unspoiled beaches along the Outer Banks are also popular spots for sunbathing and swimming. Many of the rivers in the state are great for white-water rafting, and the scenic lakes are ideal for canoeing.

Hang gliding is a popular sport in North Carolina.

Red drum and bluefish are popular catches for the surf fishers of Cape Hatteras.

QUICK FACTS

White Lake, near Elizabethtown, has been labeled "The Nation's Safest Beach." White Lake has no tides, currents, or other hazards, which might endanger the lives of swimmers.

Several popular ski resorts in North Carolina offer great downhill skiing, with a variety of runs to choose from. Among the many resorts are Ski Beech, Hawksnest, Cataloochee, and Sugar Mountain. Many of these resorts also offer cross-country skiing trails and snowshoeing trails.

Surf fishing is a popular activity in North Carolina. Surf fishers stand on the shore and use long rods to catch fish in the surf.

QUICK FACTS

Mia Hamm, from Chapel Hill, is one of the most celebrated female soccer players in the United States. At the age of 15, Mia Hamm became the youngest member of the United States national soccer team.

Meadowlark Lemon is one of the state's greatest basketball stars. Born in Wilmington, he played with the Harlem Globetrotters for 22 years. He now has his own basketball team called the Harlem All-Stars.

Stock-car racing is a very popular sport in North Carolina. The state is an important center for **NASCAR** racing, with two excellent racetracks—the Charlotte Motor Speedway and the North Carolina Speedway in Rockingham.

The Charlotte Hornets joined the National Basketball Association in 1987.

Many talented athletes have come from North Carolina. World-renowned boxer Sugar Ray Leonard was born in Wilmington. During his impressive boxing career, he won five world titles and an Olympic gold medal. Marion Jones is a track-and-field star from Wake County. She won three gold medals and two bronze medals at the 2000 Olympic Games in Sydney. No other female track-and-field star has taken home that many medals in a single Olympics. One of the best-known athletes to come out of the state is basketball superstar Michael Jordan. He spent much of his childhood in Wilmington, then later went to the University of North Carolina, where he played basketball with the Chapel Hill Tar Heels.

College basketball is one of the most popular team sports in the state. North Carolina is home to four of the leading college basketball teams in the Atlantic Coast Conference. These teams include the Chapel Hill Tar Heels, the Duke Blue Devils, the North Carolina State University Wolf Pack, and the Wake Forest University Demon Deacons. Among the state's professional teams are the Charlotte Sting, who play in the Women's National Basketball Association, the Carolina Panthers of the National Football League, and the Carolina Hurricane of the National Hockey League.

The Carolina Hurricanes play in the Entertainment and Sports Arena in Raleigh. The building can hold up to 19,000 hockey fans.

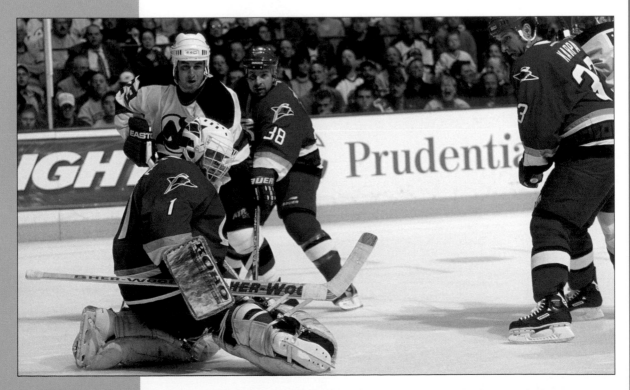

Brain Teasers

1

Which popular soft drink was first invented and served in North Carolina?

a. 7-Up

b. Coca-Cola

c. Pepsi

d. Orange Crush

Answer: c. Pepsi was first invented and served in New Bern in 1898.

2

True or False:

Snow is rarely found on Mount Mitchell, the highest peak in the eastern United States.

Answer: False. Snowstorms hit Mount Mitchell every month of the year.

3

Which great moment in baseball occurred in the town of Fayetteville?

Answer: Baseball legend Babe Ruth hit his first home run in Fayetteville in 1914.

4

North Carolina is home to the country's first known:

a. miniature golf course

b. tennis court

c. amusement park

d. indoor swimming pool

Answer: a. In 1916, James Barber, a wealthy North Carolinian, built the first miniature golf course on his estate in Pinehurst.

5 Where is the highest swinging bridge in the United States?

Answer: Perched 80 feet above the ground at Grandfather Mountain, near Linville, the Mile-High Swinging Bridge is the highest swinging bridge in the country.

6 Where in North Carolina are wild horses found?

Answer: Wild horses are found in Corolla, the northernmost town on the Outer Banks of North Carolina. The Corolla horses have inhabited this region for over 400 years.

7 Which type of natural disaster was responsible for forming Oregon Inlet and Hatteras Inlet?

Answer: In 1846, a hurricane cut two new channels in the Outer Banks, forming the Oregon and Hatteras Inlets.

8 What is North Carolina's official state beverage?

Answer: Milk was adopted as the official state beverage in 1987.

FOR MORE INFORMATION

Books

Hintz, Martin, and Stephen Hintz. *North Carolina*. Chicago: Children's Press, 1998.

Leacock, Elspeth. *The Southeast*. Washington: National Geographic Society, 2002.

Ritz, Stacy. *Hidden Carolinas*. Berkeley, CA: Ulysses Press, 1999.

Web Sites

You can also go online and have a look at the following Web sites:

North Carolina State Government
http://www.ncgov.com

North Carolina Kids Page
http://www.secretary.state.nc.us/kidspg/homepage.asp

North Carolina Tourism
http://www.visitnc.com

Some Web sites stay current longer than others. To find other North Carolina Web sites, enter search terms such as "North Carolina," "Cape Hatteras," "The Lost Colony," or any other topic you want to research.

GLOSSARY

abolished: ended

alluvial: deposits of clay or sand left behind by flowing water

carat: a unit of weight for gemstones that is equal to 0.007 ounces

carnivorous: flesh-eating

civil rights movement: the struggle in the 1950s and 1960s to provide racial equality for African Americans in the United States

conservation: the protection of wildlife and the environment

disc jockey: a person who plays recorded music on the radio

hydroelectricity: the production of electricity through water power

NASCAR: National Association for Stock Car Auto Racing

pen name: an assumed name used by a writer

pharmaceuticals: drugs and medicines

prototype: a model; the first of its kind

reservoirs: places where water is collected and stored

rural: relating to the country

segregated: forced separation and restrictions based on race

sod: blocks of grass used in the construction of early buildings

synthetic: artificial

textile: cloth, woven fabric

INDEX